# Space

Lynn M. Stone

Rourke
Publishing LLC
Vero Beach, Florida 32964

www.rourkepublishing.com

PHOTO CREDITS: All images © NASA; except page 4: © Gloria-Leigh Logan; page 12-13: © ChristianAnthony; page 14-15: © Paolo Porcellana; page 16-17: © Thomas Tuchan

Editor: Meg Greve

Cover and Interior designed by: Tara Raymo

**Library of Congress Cataloging-in-Publication Data**

Stone, Lynn M.
  Space / Lynn Stone.
    p. cm. -- (Skywatch)
  Includes index.
  ISBN 978-1-60472-296-3
  1.  Outer space--Juvenile literature.  I. Title.
  QB500.22.S73 2009
  523.1--dc22
                        2008024851


Printed in the USA

CG/CG

# Table of Contents

# Where Does Space Begin?

When you look up
in the sky, do you
wonder how close
you are to
outer space?

4

The Karman Line is the imaginary line that scientists use to divide Earth's atmosphere from space. It is 62 miles (100 kilometers) above sea level.

Outer space, or space, is the place beyond Earth's **atmosphere**.

5

The distance from where you are standing on the Earth to the edge of the atmosphere is about 62 miles (100 kilometers). That is about the same distance as if you swam across Lake Erie.

As you go higher into the atmosphere, there is less air. Outer space has no air for us to breathe.

# How Do You Get to Space?

Sputnik, the first spacecraft to **orbit** the Earth, began space exploration. Today, **astronauts** visit space on space shuttles.

Since 1981, space shuttles have been launched into space.

# What's in Space?

Because of **telescopes**, rockets, satellites, and space shuttles, we have been able to learn more about what is really in space.

## Solar System

Mercury Venus Earth Mars Jupiter Saturn Uranus Neptune

Ceres Pluto Eris

Earth is part of a group of **planets** that orbit the Sun, called the solar system.

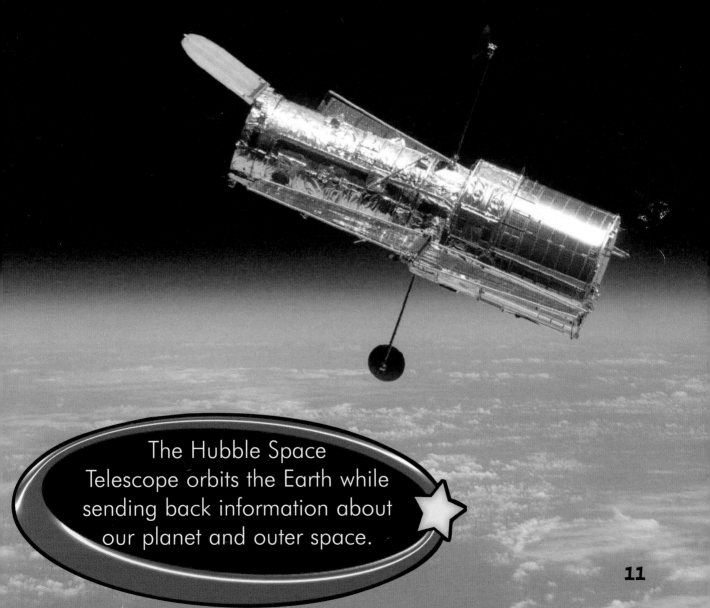

The Hubble Space Telescope orbits the Earth while sending back information about our planet and outer space.

# Asteroids and Meteoroids

Asteroids and meteoroids are pieces of rock or iron that orbit the Sun. Some meteoroids form when an asteroid breaks apart.

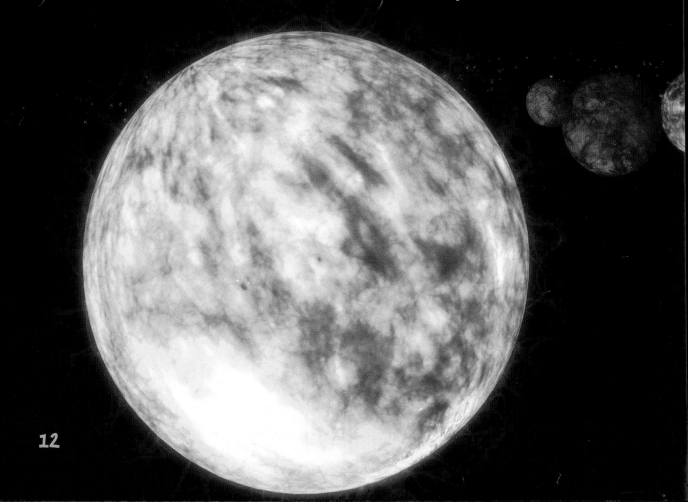

An enormous group of asteroids known as the Asteroid Belt orbit the Sun between Mars and Jupiter.

# Comets

Comets are balls of ice and dust particles that orbit the Sun. They do not always follow the same orbiting path.

The most famous comet of all is Halley's Comet. Its tail could be seen from Earth in 1986. We only get the chance to see it once every 75 years!

## Stars

Stars are huge balls of gas. Our solar system is part of the Milky Way **galaxy**. There are billions of stars in our galaxy, and billions of galaxies in our universe.

There are so many stars in outer space that we could never count them all.

# Satellites

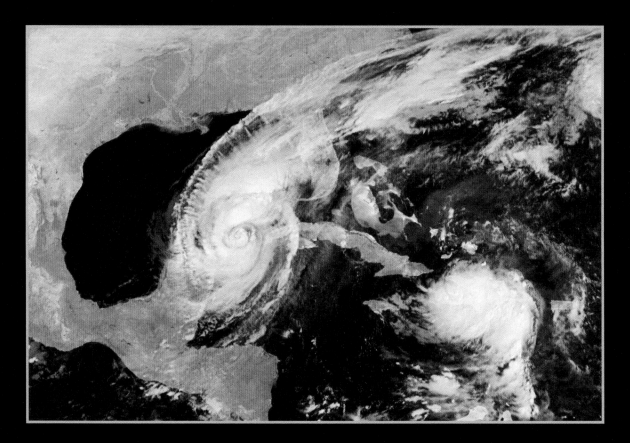

Satellites orbit the Earth, sending important information back, such as weather forecasts or pictures.

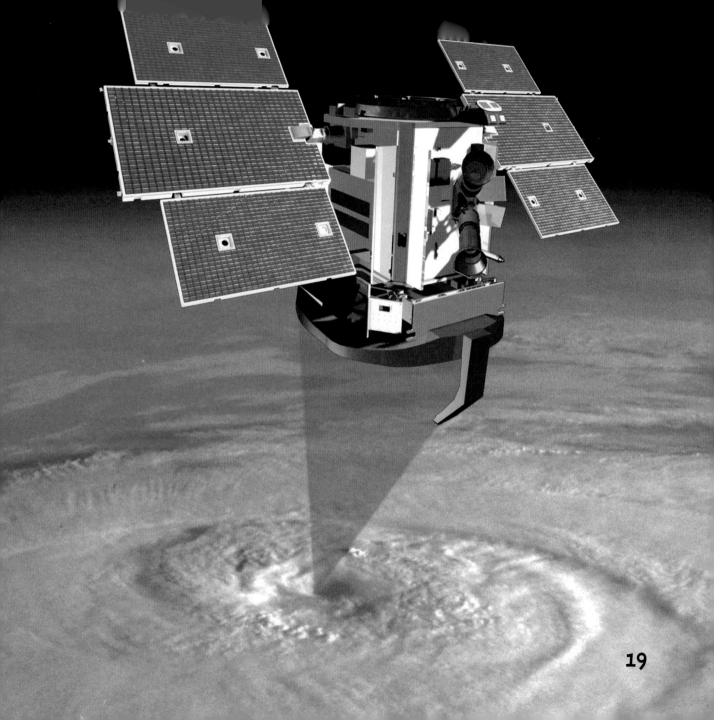

# Space Stations

The International Space Station is a permanent place in space where astronauts can live and work for months at a time.

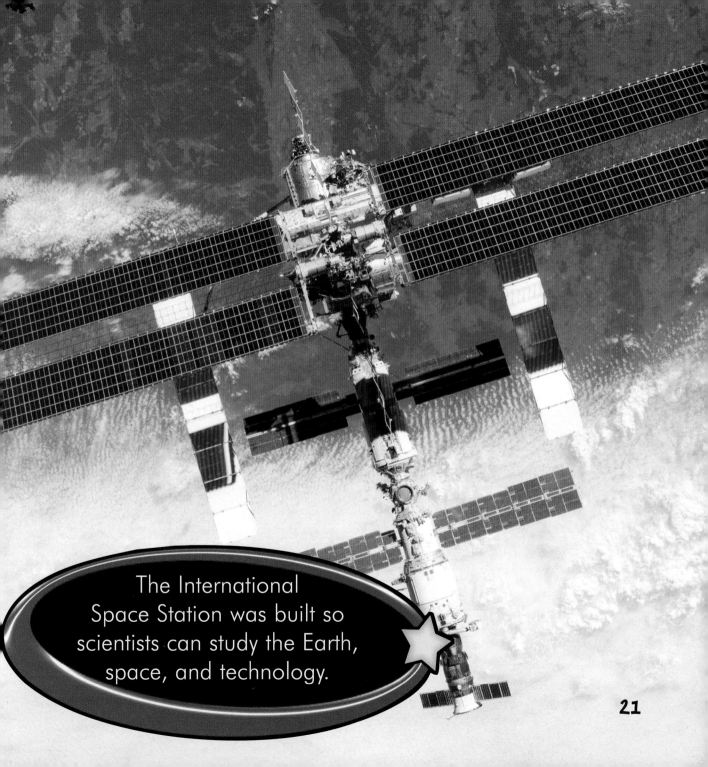

The International Space Station was built so scientists can study the Earth, space, and technology.

# Is There Life in Space?

So far, life as we know it has not been discovered outside of Earth, but the search continues.

Land rovers have been sent to Mars to study its surface and search for life.

# Glossary

**astronauts** (ASS-truh-nawts): those who fly into higher altitudes, often into outer space

**atmosphere** (AT-muhss-fihr): the mixture of gases that surround a planet

**galaxy** (GAL-uhk-see): an enormous group of stars and planets held together by gravity

**orbit** (OR-bit): move around another object in a circular path

**planets** (PLAN-its): huge, ball-shaped objects in outer space that travel around a star

**telescopes** (TEL-uh-skopes): instruments used to see objects that are very far away

# Index

## Further Reading

Bond, Peter. *Space*. DK Children, 2006.

Carruthers, Margaret W. *The Hubble Space Telescope*. Watts, 2004.

Clifford, Tim. *Space*. Rourke, 2008.

## Websites to Visit

www.discoverspace.org

www.kidsastronomy.com

http://www.frontiernet.net~kidpower/astronomy.html

## About the Author

Lynn M. Stone is a widely-published wildlife and domestic animal photographer and the author of more than 500 children's books. His book *Box Turtles* was chosen as an Outstanding Science Trade Book and Selectors' Choice for 2008 by the Science Committee of the National Science Teachers' Association and the Children's Book Council.